THE CASE OF THE ANCIENT ASTRONAUTS

by

I. J. GALLAGHER

A

Book

From

RAINTREE CHILDRENS BOOKS
Milwaukee • Toronto • Melbourne • London

Library of Congress Number: 77-10822

Art and Photo Credits

Cover illustration by Lynn Sweat.
Illustration on page 7, Culver Pictures, Inc.
Photos on pages 9, 11, and 41, Wide World Photos.
Map on page 14, "Mysteries from Forgotten Worlds," Charles Berlitz, courtesy of United States Library of Congress.
Photo on page 17, courtesy of NASA.
Photos on pages 21, 23, and 26, International Explorers Society.
Photo on page 29, John S. Flannery/Bruce Coleman.
Photo on page 31, M. P. L. Fogden/Bruce Coleman.
Photos on pages 32 and 39, Photo Trends.
Photos on pages 34 and 36, F. P. G.
Photos on pages 42, 43, 46, and 47, The American Museum of Natural History.
All photo research for this book was provided by Sherry Olan.
Every effort has been made to trace the ownership of all copyrighted material in this book and to obtain permission for its use.

Library of Congress Cataloging in Publication Data

Gallagher, I. J. 1930-
   The case of the ancient astronauts.
   SUMMARY: Investigates the possibility of early space travellers and UFO's having visited several ancient civilizations on the earth centuries ago.
   1. Civilization, Ancient—Juvenile literature. 2. Man, Prehistoric—Juvenile literature. 3. Interplanetary voyages—Juvenile literature. 4. Flying saucers—Juvenile literature. [1. Interplanetary voyages. 2. Civilization, Ancient. 3. Man, Prehistoric] I. Title.
CB156.G34   001.9′42   77-10822
ISBN 0-8172-1059-8 lib. bdg.

Manufactured in the United States of America
ISBN 0-8172-1059-8

CONTENTS

Chapter 1

WERE THERE ANCIENT ASTRONAUTS?

Do you think that unidentified flying objects (UFO's) are something new? When newspapers report stories of unknown shapes and lights in the sky, do you think it is some miracle of the modern age? If you do, think again.

According to legends, folklore, and written records, UFO's have been a mystery for thousands of years. Long ago, people simply called them other names—"flying saucers," "wheels," or "ships in the sky."

Could people in ancient times have seen flying machines? Aren't such things very new, only part of modern life on earth? Most of us think so, but that's because most of us don't know about the mystery of the ancient astronauts.

We can look for clues to this mystery in some of the earliest known reports of UFO's. The first strange flying machine we can read about looked very much like a wheel in the sky. We have this description from a man named Ezekiel in a story you can read in the Bible.

Ezekiel claimed he saw *four* living creatures come down to earth. Each creature had four different faces and four sets of wings. If the creatures had used their wings to fly, they might have been angels. That would have made Biblical sense.

But no, Ezekiel said the creatures landed on earth in a wheel-like machine. Ezekiel described it as a "wheel in the middle of a wheel." And the wheel, he said, had rings that were full of *eyes.*

The flying wheel would move with the creatures. They would leave the ground and then return. Ezekiel said it came and went in "a flash

Ezekiel with the winged creatures he said came down from the sky. Here they are shown with only one of the four faces they each had.

of lightning." He doesn't explain whether the creatures were inside or outside the wheel, but he found it a fearful sight.

Ezekiel had an explanation for what he saw. He claimed that a greater being was trying to reach him. This experience had deep religious meaning for Ezekiel. Of course, a modern-day "UFO watcher" might say something very different. To such a person, this might have been the visit to earth of people from other planets. The "wheels" would be a flying saucer and the "eyes" in the rings would be windows. The spinning motion would make the saucer appear to have several rings or "a wheel within a wheel." *Could Ezekiel have been the first UFO eyewitness?*

Thousands of years after Ezekiel, a famous astronomer, E. W. Maunder, reported a strange cigar-shaped object in the sky over England. This was in 1882. He and his fellow astronomers at the Royal Observatory in Greenwich, England, were able to watch the flying object through a telescope. They made notes about what they saw.

The strange object appeared quite suddenly out of nowhere. The astronomers described it as looking very much like a "cigar" or "torpedo." They agreed it moved "too fast for a cloud and too slow for a meteor." The object had a definite shape with a dark center.

Dr. Maunder saw this mysterious object many years before earth people had invented any kind of flying machine. It could not have been launched from earth. What was the object the astronomers saw? No one knows to this day.

Some UFO watchers think that flying saucers are launched from a large mother spaceship. The mother ship makes the long journey across space from its home to earth. Then it sends out a smaller flying saucer to observe the earth more closely. Most experts picture the mother ship as being cigar-shaped. It might be compared to a "flying boxcar." This was an airplane used dur-

In a practice session, these paratroopers jump from a "flying boxcar," designed to carry great loads of cargo or troops.

ing wartime to carry large machines, such as tanks, and other military equipment into battle.

There were other UFO reports in the late 1800s. Another cigar-shaped object was seen over the United States in November, 1869. According to C. B. Colby, an eyewitness, a large, dark, "cigar-shaped object with stubby wings" was seen by thousands of people going home from work in San Francisco, California.

A few hours later, people north of San Francisco reported seeing the very same object. They couldn't call it an airplane. Airplanes hadn't even been invented. They didn't know what to call it. The object returned almost a week later. It moved steadily in the sky against the wind, which meant it had to be powered by some kind of energy.

The cigar-shape in the sky kept returning. During the next four months, it was sighted in Nebraska, Missouri, Minnesota, and Wisconsin. On April 10, 1870, thousands of people in Chicago, Illinois, saw it. People reported seeing it during the next ten days. Then, it disappeared. What was it? Where did it come from? No one has ever found out. Why did it come to

Is this UFO, photographed in Japan in 1937, like the one seen in the United States?

earth? Were humans being studied by creatures from outer space?

UFO watchers tell of hundreds of UFO sightings over the centuries. Reports of "wheels of light," "great ships in the sky," and "chariots" fill the pages of history. Scientists often do not accept the reports of UFO watchers as fact. Scientists want real proof of what actually happened, and no one has ever captured a flying saucer or an outer space creature. A storm of argument rages between those who believe the UFO's are visitors from other worlds and those who believe UFO's are really *ordinary* flying objects.

Have astronauts from other worlds visited our planet? If there is life on other planets, can it be so far ahead of us that space people have been visiting us since our ancient past?

There are more and more scientists investigating the case of the ancient astronauts. You will find all kinds of detectives—map makers, explorers, archaeologists, mathematicians—searching for clues in *The Case of the Ancient Astronauts*.

Chapter 2

※

ANCIENT MAPS: WHERE DID THEY COME FROM?

There is a map of the earth that presents some important but puzzling clues for the case of the ancient astronauts. It is called the *Piri Reis Map*, and UFO detectives are studying it very carefully.

Admiral Piri Reis was in the Turkish Navy in the early 19th century. He drew a map of the earth that was found by historians in 1929 in Istanbul, Turkey. The map shows *exact* outlines of the earth's continents, with good details of mountains, plains, and rivers.

The odd thing about the Piri Reis Map is that it shows a view of the earth that can be seen only from a great height. It is almost like a photo taken from the air. Some people now think it was actually made by ancient astronauts. *And there are good reasons for them to think so.*

The Piri Reis map. Who had the knowledge, so many years ago, to draw such accurate maps?

First of all, the center point of the Piri Reis Map is Egypt. All points within 5,000 miles of Cairo are drawn with the right shape. Lands beyond this distance, however, such as South America, Australia, and Antarctica, seem drawn out of shape. But this is how these lands would look when seen from high above the ground over Egypt.

Another clue is the appearance of Antarctica on the map. The coast of Antarctica was not explored until 1820. Its mountain ranges were not discovered until 1952. Yet, both are drawn on the Piri Reis Map. How was this possible? How could Admiral Reis have had all this information in the early 1800s?

Admiral Piri Reis wrote on his map that he pieced it together from "ancient maps" that date back to around 330 B.C. in Egypt. Professor Charles H. Hapgood, an expert on ancient maps, discovered that the ancient Egyptian priests had been very careful to store all their knowledge of geography in maps. But the priests weren't the original map makers. They claimed they had gotten the maps from "The Ancient Peoples." Who were these "Ancient" people? Did *they* have the advanced instruments needed to make such maps? Did they have spacecraft from which they photographed the earth?

Professor Hapgood and mathematician Richard W. Strachan compared modern satellite maps of the earth with the Piri Reis Map. Amazingly, an *Apollo 8* satellite photograph looks very much like the Reis map. In 1957 a U.S. Navy map and chart maker, Father Lineham, said the ancient maps were exact in almost every detail. You can see how some people would add up these clues.

Some UFO watchers think the earth was visited by spacemen in ancient times, just as they think happens today. One expert, Dr. George Hunt Williamson, believes UFO's appear over the earth just before some great change happens on our planet. He feels the appearance of UFO's is really a warning to earth people. Williamson wonders if the increased number of UFO's that have been seen since World War II are really warning us of a great change in the near future.

Ideas like Williamson's often trigger other people's imaginations. Many wonder if our atomic explosions have had effects elsewhere in

In this satellite photo you can clearly see North and South America (upper left and center) and the West Coast of Africa (upper right).

the universe. Have our bombs upset faraway civilizations we know nothing about?

Others wonder if beings from other planets are waiting for the right moment to take over the earth. Or do they fear an invasion from *us?* Who are these space people and where are they from?

UFO watcher Gavin Gibbons believes that space beings come from a tenth planet that exploded. Our solar system has nine known planets circling our sun. The *asteroids*, a group of small planets between Mars and Jupiter, might at one time have been a tenth planet. Gibbons wonders if a tenth planet was shattered into these smaller bodies in an atomic blast. Could some of its people have survived in spaceships? Could the survivors have gone to another planet to live? Could these space survivors be watching the earth to save it from a similar atomic blast?

There are those who think the people from the lost continent of Atlantis flew in airships called *vimanas* more than 11,000 years ago. These vimanas could be called the first flying saucers. Atlantis was thought to be an ancient continent in the Atlantic Ocean. After several great earthquakes and tidal waves about 11,500 years ago, Atlantis is thought to have sunk into the ocean. It is believed that some of the Atlanteans escaped to Egypt and countries to the east. Others may have escaped west to the Americas.

The Atlantean people were thought to be highly advanced in science. Were "The Ancient Peoples" who gave maps to the Egyptian priests really people who escaped from Atlantis? Perhaps they mapped the earth from above, flying in their vimanas.

If the ancient astronauts existed, they would have seen some unusual sights while flying over the earth. Surely, they would have looked twice at some strange ground markings in the Nazca Valley of Peru.

Chapter 3

THE LINES OF NAZCA

For the next clues in our mystery we must travel to Peru in South America. There, at the foot of the Andes Mountains, a dry, sandy plain is marked with lines that look very much like runways at an airport. Archaeologists say that the early Peruvians, called Incas, carved the lines as roadways. Other scientists say that they were not roadways but landing strips for ancient astronauts.

We are over the Nazca Plains in Peru. Approaching by plane we can see straight tracks of white carved in the earth. They run side by side.

When seen from the air, these lines carved in the
earth form a hummingbird.

There are other lines crossing these tracks. Between the tracks are outlines of huge figures—spiders, monkeys, and birds. The figures are so large, they cannot be seen except from the air.

The Nazca Plain is a 37-mile strip of flat ground covered with rust-colored rocks. No plants grow here. The lines on the plain were made by removing the rocks from the surface. This left a yellowish-white soil which stands out against the brown, rocky desert.

The Inca markings at Nazca have survived the centuries because it rains only 20 minutes each year on this plain. The ancient artists who designed the lines must have had a large plan in mind. One figure stretches out over 275 yards! Erich von Daniken, in his book *Gods From Outer Space*, says these lines were used as a landing field by ancient astronauts.

Archaeologist Maria Reiche disagrees with von Daniken's idea that the Plain of Nazca was an airstrip for spacemen. She doesn't believe they landed there to carry out their mission. But she agrees that the lines were not roads. Maria Reiche suggests the markings were designs of the heavens. She thinks they were probably ancient calendars.

Gerald S. Hawkins decided to examine the calendar theory. He took measures to see if the markings related to the stars. He tried to prove that the changing positions of the sun, moon, and stars over the markings would have served as a calendar for the Incas. Hawkins put his information into a computer. The computer found that this theory didn't work. The markings are

Maria Reiche is shown here with Jim Woodman (left) and Julian Knott, who came to Nazca to photograph the famous lines.

not a calendar. Hawkins, however, couldn't come up with any new answers of his own.

Another expert, Jim Woodman, believes the lines were used by ancient Inca balloonists. In his book about Woodman, *Mystery in Peru: The Lines of Nazca,* Dr. David McMullen explores this idea. He wonders if the Incas, 2,000 years ago, invented the first hot-air balloons. The book offers evidence to prove the Incas knew about flying. But did they do this alone? Or were they taught by ancient astronauts?

On one point all experts agree. The pattern of markings on the Plain of Nazca can be seen only from the air. The builders must have planned the design and drawn it on a smaller scale first. Otherwise they couldn't have moved the right number of rocks to etch all of those perfect designs in the sand.

In his book *Gods From Outer Space,* Erich von Daniken makes a strong argument that the Plain of Nazca was a spaceport. He supports this idea by reporting other strange markings he has discovered in South America. He had seen a carving of a giant candelabra shining on the high, red cliffs above the Bay of Pisco. This bay is on the Pacific coast of Peru, not far from Nazca. Why was this gigantic, 820-foot-high drawing made? What was it used for?

That's what von Daniken set out to learn. He asked a fisherman to take him to the cliff walls by boat. The first thing he discovered was that the drawing really couldn't be seen too well from the water. For that reason, von Daniken figured it didn't mark a harbor. This proved to be true when the fisherman wouldn't take his boat into shore because of sharp reefs.

Von Daniken also noticed that the drawing pointed up to the sky rather than down to the sea. In order to look at it closely, von Daniken waded to the shore and walked through the hot sand to the cliff itself. He measured and photographed the drawing. He found that it was made of white blocks as hard as granite stuck into the cliffside. The blocks were so firmly attached to the hard sand, he couldn't knock one loose. The white stones shone against the dark cliffside so that they could be seen from very far away. But the story doesn't end there.

Von Daniken checked his directions and found the drawing seemed to point toward the

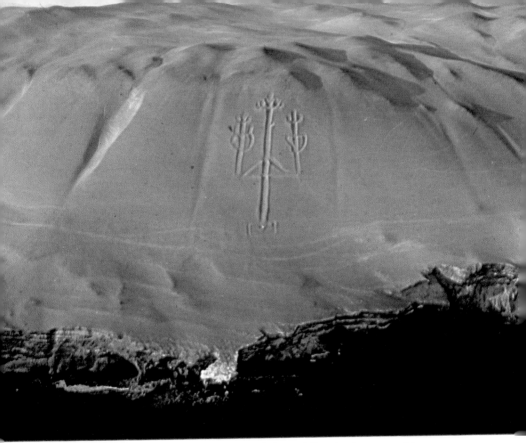

Was the 840-foot Candelabra of the Andes meant to
point the way to Nazca?

Plain of Nazca. It was about 200 miles away. Von
Daniken decided the drawing was a landmark,
pointing the way to the airstrip.

But von Daniken didn't stop following the
direction that the candelabra marked when he
reached Nazca. He kept going in a straight line
past the Nazca Valley. At a place called the
Plateau of El Enladrillado in northern Chile, he
found another possible landing strip. This one
was marked out by huge stone blocks.

Von Daniken heard of another giant figure in Chile. This was a 330-foot-high robot, outlined in volcanic stones. The robot's body was rectangular and its legs dropped straight down. Its thin neck supported a head with 12 antennae. From hip to thigh, triangular fins (like wings of supersonic fighters) were attached to the body on both sides. Was this robot made by men? Some experts believe it was the work of beings from another planet. How would ancient artists know what a robot looked like? Was the robot an ancient astronaut in space clothing?

No one is sure why these huge landmarks were built. None of the theories has really been proven. Maybe you agree with von Daniken that ancient astronauts used these markings to land on earth. Perhaps these astronauts will return. Those who believe in UFO's think space people may have already returned. Did these people ever stop at the ancient Mayan cities in Central America? That's our next stop in the hunt for clues in the case of the ancient astronauts.

Chapter 4

MAYAN MYSTERIES

In the dense forests of Central America lived an ancient people called the Mayas. Intelligent and civilized, the Mayas built huge cities, beautiful temples, and enormous pyramids in the tropical jungles of Mexico, Guatemala, Honduras, and British Honduras. This building began about 2000 B.C., and continued for over 2,800 years.

Suddenly, in 869 A.D., the Mayas stopped building. Mysteriously, they left their temples and pyramids unguarded. These buildings became overgrown by the dense jungle and lay hidden for centuries. Only in recent years have archaeologists started to uncover the mysteries of the Mayan past. They are trying to find out why the Mayas built these amazing places in the middle of a hot, snake-filled jungle. Archaeologists are also trying to solve the question of why the Mayas stopped their building so suddenly.

The Mayan Temple of the Inscriptions at Palenque, Mexico.

Are the ancient Mayan cities still inhabited? Dr. George Hunt Williamson thinks it is possible. He says that since 1955, UFO's have been sighted in the area of the ancient cities. He wonders if astronauts are seeking old records still buried there. Might there even be ancient astronauts still living in these "lost" cities?

Religion shaped the Mayas' lives. Their religious beliefs give us some clues to the meaning of their monuments. The Mayas believed in the stars. They believed that numbers had special, magical meanings. Numbers even became gods. Each day was a god, as well as a number.

Archaeologists have figured out that the Mayan calendar began August 11, 3114 B.C. What was the importance of that date which was long before the beginning of Mayan history? Might it have been the date of an arrival from the skies—perhaps the coming of the Mayan gods? This would be similar to our present calendar dates that start with the birth of Christ.

The Mayan calendar estimated the year at 365.2420 days. Modern scientists have computed the figure at 365.2422 days. The Mayas' accuracy in this is astounding. The Mayas also *knew* that a year on the planet Venus lasted 584

A calendar stone, 12 feet in diameter, carved by the Aztecs, who lived after the Mayas.

days. They worshipped Venus as a god. Through astronomy, they figured out that the paths of the sun, moon, and Venus would bring them together in a straight line every 37,960 days. On those days, Mayan myths claimed, the gods would come to earth to their "great resting place." If the Mayas were expecting the ancient gods to return to earth, it would explain their keen interest in the calendar and astronomy.

31

The Mayan building of pyramids and temples was directly connected to the expected return of their gods. Every 52 years, a fixed number of steps had to be completed on their pyramids. Each stone had its relation to the calendar. The Mayas' frantic building seems to have been a race against the date their gods would come back to them.

A pyramid in the ancient Mayan city of Chichen Itzá.

Perhaps when the gods did not return to the temples, the Mayas were disappointed. Would that be an explanation of why the people might have turned against the priests, thrown away their tools, and vanished into the jungle? This may be the reason the Mayas stopped building.

Modern people find it hard to believe that the Mayas knew so much about astronomy and mathematics. But it's true. The Mayas developed an accurate calendar and a complex *hieroglyphic* (word pictures) writing. Erich von Daniken suggests that unknown visitors—an ancient space people from the skies—gave the Mayas their scientific knowledge.

The Mayas left records of their history carved in stone. Their picture-writing is all we have left to fill in the clues to the mystery of the ancient astronauts.

*   *   *   *

The mystery we seek to solve begins and, so far, ends with a single question—*were there ancient astronauts?* Were there visitors who flew through space, from other worlds, to land on the

Many clues to the mysterious past of the Mayas can be found in
their carved stone statues.

planet earth? Was it from such visitors that the ancient civilizations on earth learned science and mathematics? Was it for such visitors that ancient people carved markings in the earth?

We have still uncovered too few clues to answer these questions. But each year new clues are dug up. For example, a Mayan picture, carved in stone, has been found. It may be just the clue we are after.

A stone carving of a Mayan god—Kuhumatz —was found in the ancient city of Palenque. In the carving a man is shown sitting on an object that looks like a rocketship. The object is pointed in front. A flame shoots from its tail. The man is leaning forward. He seems to be turning controls of some kind. He is wearing short pants, a broad belt, and a jacket with a high collar. His clothing has bands at the arms and legs, fitting much like a modern spacesuit. The headgear has tubes and something that looks like antennae on top. *Was this an ancient astronaut?*

Mayan stone writings tell stories about their gods. One legend describes a god who came from a "country of the rising sun." He wore a white robe and a beard. He taught people the sciences and left them with wise laws. The legend says that he left the earth on a flying ship to the morning star, but he promised to return.

The tomb of the great Mayan ruler Pascal was found in southern Mexico in 1952. A five-ton limestone lid seals his coffin. Carved in the stone lid is a picture of Pascal. He is lying in a curled-up position. Erich von Daniken com-

Could the carved figure on the lid of Pascal's coffin be an "Ancient Astronaut"?

pares Pascal's position in the stone carving to that of modern-day astronauts in a space capsule. Pascal's hands seem to be ready to touch or to hold some objects. Von Daniken says the markings on the bottom of the carving look like flames and gases that would come from the exhaust of a spaceship. Is Pascal pictured making his trip to the gods?

More clues, more theories, but still no real proof that there were ancient astronauts. Our hunt goes on, and to find more clues we must now journey to a tiny island in the great Pacific Ocean.

Chapter 5

LAND OF THE BIRD MEN

Far west of Chile, across the Pacific Ocean, stand the stone statues of Easter Island. Hundreds of these giant statues stare with scorn at visitors to the small island. And the visitors simply stare back, amazed that some ancient people could have moved these huge stones—some more than 60 feet tall and weighing over 80 tons —distances up to 10 miles.

The statues are of people. They are frightening-looking. They look nothing like the Polynesian people who have lived on Easter

A giant stone head on the slope of the volcano Rano Raraku
on Easter Island.

Island since ancient times. Who, then, do the statues look like?

The Easter Island statues are different from all others found in the world. Father Sebastian Englert, a priest on the island for 34 years, says the statues were known by the name of *aringa ora*. This name means "living faces." But *whose* faces?

One expert, the explorer Thor Heyerdahl, found hundreds of simple, stone, carving tools lying in the stone quarries when he visited Easter Island in 1955. It appeared to him that the ancient stone cutters had thrown down their tools and walked off the job. No one is certain why.

Father Englert, the Easter Island priest, says that a tribal war was one possible explanation of why the stone carving stopped. Erich von Daniken suggests a different reason. His theory is that a small group of intelligent beings from another planet showed the islanders how to make the statues with advanced tools.

Von Daniken does not think it was possible for the islanders to chisel the statues with the simple tools that were found in the quarry. Nor could he see any way for the ancient people to

This huge statue with its odd hat silently stands guard
on Easter Island.

These bird men of Easter Island are carved into rocks.

have moved the massive stones to their sites across the island.

Von Daniken thinks that the indistinct shapes on some of the statues' heads are helmet-type hats, like the ones astronauts wear. Perhaps the natives dropped their tools and returned to their carefree lives when the beings from space left. Maybe the statues were made to look like the ancient astronauts.

Easter Island has been called by many names. Today, the islanders call it the "Land of

Small statues of the bird men were also carved in wood.

the Bird Men." An old legend says that flying men landed there and lighted fires in ancient times. This legend is seen in ancient rock carvings of the bird men.

Easter Island may or may not provide more clues in the case of the ancient astronauts. It certainly raises more *questions.* How *were* the giant rocks moved and carved without machines and with only the simplest tools? What truth, if any, lies in the "bird men" legends? Who *do* the statues look like? Many of these questions are discussed by Miriam Weiss Meyer in her book, *The Blind Guards of Easter Island.*

Chapter 6

THE SKY PEOPLE

The Ainu people of northern Japan claim their ancestors were space people. On a hill in the Saru River Valley, a monument marks the spot where the first Ainu are said to have landed.

The Ainu live on Hokkaido, the northern-most island of Japan. The Ainu themselves are a mystery. They are not like the people in the countries around them. The Ainu do not have oriental eyes. They have round, dark-brown eyes with curling lashes.

This Ainu woman has been tatooed with a mustache in keeping with Ainu tradition.

The Ainu language is a puzzle. It is completely different from Japanese, and it has no written form. The younger Ainu have adopted Japanese as their language, moving further and further from their old Ainu culture. Without written records we have only the stories told from generation to generation as a history of these mysterious people. And the Ainu stories all say they are the descendants of "people from the sky."

* * * *

For centuries, humans have been puzzled about their own beginnings. Today we live in a world filled with unsolved mysteries. *The Case of the Ancient Astronauts* has told about only a few of these mysteries—statues with space helmets, nameless gods with stone faces, line drawings seen only from the sky, aerial maps made centuries before humans learned to fly, and ancient writings that cannot be read.

Before ceremonial bear slaughter, an Ainu man demonstrates the bow dance.

In the future, humans will probably reach other planets and may find intelligent life there. The sightings of UFO's will cease to be a mystery if astronauts from outer space make themselves known. Then, perhaps, we will know if *they* were the ancient sky gods.

The Case of the Ancient Astronauts is an unfinished story. The detective work is incomplete. We are still uncertain if there were ancient astronauts and who they were. Maybe someday *you* will be the scientist who finds evidence that they once did live—*and may still be living now.*